Learning Leadership From
—NEHEMIAH—

DAVE KRAFT
DAVEKRAFT.ORG

www.davekraft.org

Cover design by www.jrbdesignco.com
Book layout by Kristin White www.fourohseven.com
Published by MultiplyLeaders   www.multiplyleaders.co
Thanks to Karla Scharfinski, Mike Sherman, Chad Myers, Larry Bennett Sr. and others who were readers and editors, helping to bring out the fullness of this work.

DEDICATION

I have been a Christian for 55 years and in pastoral ministry for 48 years, both with churches and para-local church organizations. I have been blessed to have many leaders pour into my life over these many years.

I want to thank Lloyd Deem for being the first link in the chain in my becoming a Christian when we worked at the post office together. I am grateful to Roy and Alta Davis for being my earliest teachers and mentors. Paul Stanley (Navigator leader) took me under his wing when Susan and I lived in Colorado Springs and both believed in me and mentored me in leadership. Pastor Mike Coppersmith was my Pastor for ten years when we were at Our Savior's Community Church in Palm Springs. Mike modeled for me what godly and consistent leadership looks like.

My wife Susan has always been an encouragement to me and told me over and over that I needed to get one more book out there. Here it is, Susan.

Most of all, I thank my Lord Jesus for saving me, gifting me and calling me to ministry as a leader developer.

CONTENTS

FOREWORD

It has been my privilege to know Dave Kraft for nearly thirty years. We spent ten of those years serving together on the same ministry staff of a local church. As the senior pastor of that church, I saw firsthand Dave's vision, passion, commitment and daily application of the leadership principles that you read about in this book. Those ten years were like a classroom for me, as God used Dave to impart into my life these leadership lessons from Nehemiah. My life as a leader, and the lives of many other leaders in our church, was transformed by these lessons.

Every day you have a choice to make in your walk with God and your walk with other people. You can choose to be a thermometer or you can choose to be a thermostat. Thermometers simply indicate what is going on around them. Thermostats, on the other hand, influence what is going on around them. By God's grace, Dave Kraft—like Nehemiah and all the great leaders of the Bible—has chosen to be a thermostat.

I'm confident that the Holy Spirit will use this short but significant book by Dave to help you and many others make that same choice.

As you read what follows, you'll be reminded that Christian leadership—like Christ Himself—is all about the heart. So, let me encourage you to read and discuss these lessons prayerfully, not just with your mind but also with your heart. Ask God to transform you into the influential and transformative leader He made you to be. Because, now more than ever, this world needs more Nehemiahs!

Pastor Mike Coppersmith
Georgetown, Texas

INTRODUCTION

When it comes to the subject of leadership in action, one of my favorite Old Testament characters is Nehemiah. In his story we see every facet of leadership lived out. I admire the depth of his prayer life, his love for God, and his sterling character. I admire his courage in the face of crises, his willingness to make tough decisions, his perseverance to stand for what is right, and his candor in dealing with people. He is a man of prayer, a man of faith, a man of vision, a man of courage, and a man of action. We find him praying, watching, working, and warring. He's my kind of leader.

I have studied my way through Nehemiah with two groups of leaders, and each study was insightful and challenging. It is a book rich in leadership principles. The late J. Sidlow Baxter says about the lessons in Nehemiah, "There is no winning without working, no opportunity without opposition, no triumph without trouble, no victory without vigilance."

In the first chapter, we find him receiving a vision from God. From that point on, we watch as he casts the vision, recruits to the vision, and works tirelessly to insure that the vision happens. I can't think of a single aspect of exemplary leadership that is not lived out in this man and recorded in this book.

What I would like to do in the chapters ahead is to focus on some leadership principles we see in Nehemiah's life. We will not do an expository study on the book of Nehemiah, nor a character study on his life. I will purposely avoid historical information that might be interesting, but not germane to my objective of sharing leadership principles that I have found instructive. I will also offer questions at the end of each chapter to stimulate your thinking as you consider your leadership role in light of these principles.

01

Christian Leaders are deeply concerned about the fulfillment of God's plan and purpose. In dependence on Him, they do something about it.

As the curtain goes up in the first chapter of the book, we are introduced to Nehemiah who was taken captive and is now serving the king of Persia as his cupbearer. He inquires about the state of Jerusalem and the Jewish people living there who were left behind or had returned from captivity. What he heard was devastating. His first response was not to draw up a strategic plan, nor begin enlisting people for the cause. Rather, he began by weeping, mourning, fasting and praying for many days. He confessed sin, reminded God of His promises and sensed a call.

Leadership always begins with God; the glorious truth that He's up to something and wants me to be a part of it. True spiritual leadership is getting on my heart what God has on His. As Henry Blackaby has stated, "I want to know where God is at work and how I can join Him in that work."[1]

It was Robert Kennedy who said, "Some people see what is and ask why? Others see what could be and ask why not?"

After reading about Nehemiah and his response to the news, I wrote this in my journal.

"Lord, break my heart with the things that break your heart. Do I mourn, weep and seek you over the state of the church and the Great Commission? Am I deeply concerned with what concerns you, or am I passively asleep in the light?"

I am challenged by Nehemiah's humility. He gets with God before getting into action, and starts with God's character and promises.

QUESTIONS TO PONDER

What impresses you about Nehemiah's response to the report he received?

What does it mean to have on your heart what God has on his?

What is preventing you from being dependent on God?

In what way do you avoid asking the difficult questions as a way of avoiding dependence upon God for a big answer?

02

Leaders have big dreams. They have divinely inspired desires birthed from dissatisfaction with the status quo.

Nothing significant starts happening until somebody starts dreaming. Every accomplishment started off first as an idea in somebody's mind. It started off as a dream. It started off as a vision, a goal. The first task of leadership is to hear from God and let him form a vision. If you don't set the vision, you're not the leader. In reality, whoever is establishing the vision and goals in your church or group is the real leader.

A church, group, or organization will never outgrow its vision and the vision of a group of people will never outgrow the vision of its leader.[2]

In chapter one of this marvelous book, we see Nehemiah receiving some bad news, which sends him to his knees in confession, prayer, and brokenness. Rising from his knees he seems to be (from that moment on) a man of destiny. He has a strong sense of calling to do something about what he has just heard. Visionary leaders share a deep unhappiness with the way things are. There is a burden, a sense of call to change the status quo. The leader wants to be a part of building a new and different future. I see this in Nehemiah.

In Nehemiah 2:1-8, he presents his BHAG (Big Hairy Audacious Goals), coined by Jim Collins in his book "Good To Great." He articulates his faith-filled requests to the king with a trembling but confident heart and gets what he requests. It was William Carey who said, "Attempt great things for God. Expect great things from God." Nehemiah did exactly that.

I recently read the account of Joseph. When he was young, he had a dream that his father and brothers were bowing down to him. This did not sit well with them and in response his brothers say, "Here comes that dreamer...we'll see what becomes of all his dreams." (Genesis 37:19-20) At this point they sold him into slavery in Egypt and thought they were through with him. Imagine their shock when years later that very same dream came true; they saw first-hand what happens when God gives a dream.

In Genesis 42:9 we read, "And Joseph remembered the dreams that he had dreamed of them..." Perhaps this was an "aha moment" for Joseph when he connected the dots of God's handiwork in his life. Many of us have had (at one time or another) crazy ideas and wild dreams. Some of them occurred while we were in the shower. What separates leaders of action is the leader who steps out of the shower and does something about it. In Joseph's case it was God who never let the dream die, as it was God's idea to start with. God uses all the seemingly unfortunate circumstances in Joseph's life and the dream is fulfilled.

This, coupled with the account of Nehemiah's vision of what God wanted to do, gives me renewed hope. I am reassessing some of my earlier dreams and desires to see if they are from God and if He still wants to see them come true. Pastor Andy Stanley reminds us, "What God initiates he orchestrates." If God gave the dream, he will see it through to fruition. He will work out all the details.

After reading the second chapter of Nehemiah, I wrote in my journal: "Lord, don't let me dream and think too small. I want to be a change agent and see what could be, not what already is."

QUESTIONS TO PONDER

What about the dreams you once had? In what way may you have forgotten about those God-given dreams? What would it look like for you to begin believing the Lord once again?

What current vision and dream does your church have that adds excitement and joy to the daily work? What benefit would your team have by getting away to revisit and rethink your vision and dreams?

As you think about your dreams, what can you do to begin casting that vision and bringing others on board to travel with you?

03
Leaders have clarity about what they want to see happen.

We are learning from Nehemiah. He has a burden from the Lord. He receives a vision about what he is to do. He casts the vision. He carries out the vision. It all begins with God in chapter one. For the Christian leader, God must be the beginning, middle, and end of the vision.

Eugene Peterson in *The Message* renders Philippians 1:6 as follows: "There has never been the slightest doubt in my mind that the God who started this great work in you would keep at it and bring it to a *flourishing finish* on the very day Christ Jesus appears." God will bring our salvation to a flourishing finish and also desires to bring the vision he births in us to a flourishing finish!

A number of years ago I picked up a used book titled, "*If You Don't Know Where You're Going, You'll Probably End Up Somewhere Else.*"[4] The title of this excellent book contains an important lesson. I believe that a leader needs to have clarity about where to go. Generally, followers are not motivated to sign up for ambiguity! Experience has taught me that there are three things that attract people to a leader: Character, Compassion, and Clarity.

In Nehemiah 2:4, the king asked Nehemiah, "What are you requesting?" I would paraphrase that as: What do you have in mind? What is it you intend to do? What exactly is it you want to accomplish? Nehemiah was prepared with a clear response. From the first information he received in chapter one until the question from the king was asked in chapter two, four months had passed. Nehemiah had time to think, envision, and pray. He was ready. "So I prayed to the God of heaven. And I said to the king, If it pleases the king, and if your servant has found favor in your sight, that you send me to Judah, to the city of my fathers' graves, that I may rebuild it." (Nehemiah 2:4-5) Exactly what he wanted to accomplish was clear from the start. Nehemiah didn't have all the details down, but the end-product was solidly planted by God in his mind and heart—to see the city of Jerusalem rebuilt, starting with the wall. Later in chapter two when he cast the vision, he was equally clear and precise as to what he wanted to do. In Nehemiah 2:17 we read,

> "Then I said to them, you see the trouble we are in; Jerusalem lies in ruins and its gates have been burned with fire. Come, let us rebuild the wall of Jerusalem and we will no longer be a disgrace."

As I work with leaders and churches I am constantly asking questions concerning their vision. Who are you? What are you all about? What has God birthed in your heart regarding the future? Many don't have any answers. A leader's ability to move forward and have others join him on the journey will be proportionate to a clear sense of where he is headed and what, with God's help, he wants to see happen.

Someone has observed that what gets measured gets done. When a vision is clear, you have a way of measuring progress. You can determine if you are accomplishing it or not. When a vision is clear, it is a powerful motivator and a significant morale lifter among those banding together with a leader. When a company, group, team, or church is casting vision, it needs to be as specific as possible. When a sports team begins a season, the coach will often declare exactly what the goal is for the year. The people on the team know specifically what they are shooting for. It might be to be national champions; it could be to have a winning season. It might be to make it to the play-offs; it might be a rebuilding year.

I recently re-watched the movie, *"Miracle on Ice."* The U.S. hockey team coach had his vision clear from the beginning. It was to beat the Soviet Union; something that hadn't happened in 20 years. There was no doubt among the team members; every man knew exactly what they were all about. The vision needed to be a stretch, a challenge, but not a total impossibility. We will see, as we continue with Nehemiah, that the vision before them would challenge them to the max, but was doable with God's help.

Leader! Vision caster! Dreamer of dreams! What exactly are you all about? What has God called you to accomplish? What is it that burns in your heart? If you don't know where you're going, you'll probably end up somewhere else!

QUESTIONS TO PONDER

How can a leader obtain clarity regarding a vision?

What are some disadvantages of having a general vision with little clarity or specificity?

What is the difference between desire, hope, and vision?

04

**Leaders inspire and motivate
followers to action in order to
achieve a God-given vision.**

We come to chapter two in the odyssey of this man of God. He has prayed and received a God-given, God-size vision from the Lord. He has solicited permission from the king to make the journey back to Jerusalem to begin rebuilding the wall. In chapter two he surveys the situation at night with a few choice men and in verses 17 and 18 we read:

> "Then I said to them, 'You see the trouble we are in: Jerusalem lies in ruins and its gates have been burned with fire. Come, let us rebuild the wall of Jerusalem and we will no longer be in disgrace; I also told them about the gracious hand of my God upon me, and what the king had said to me. They replied, 'Let us start rebuilding.' So they began this good work."

In Harvard professor John Kotter's excellent book, *Leading Change*, he mentions an eight-fold process for a change agent:

1. Establishing a Sense of Urgency
2. Creating the Guiding Coalition
3. Developing a Vision and Strategy
4. Communicating the Change Vision
5. Empowering employees for Broad-Based Action
6. Generating Short-Term Wins
7. Consolidating Gains and Producing More Change
8. Anchoring New Approaches in the Culture

Now, Nehemiah never went to Harvard, never knew John Kotter, and never read any of his books, but he carries out this process in full. Here in chapter two, *he establishes a sense of urgency* by saying, "You see the trouble we are in ..." He shares both the problem and the solution. A problem without a solution is just a complaint. It is so easy to see the problem and complain. "Woe is me. Ain't it awful? Whatever are we going to do?"

A leader is a person who has a vision from God, firmly believes in that vision, and doesn't move toward its fulfillment alone. Real leaders possess the ability to get others motivated about this new idea. They know the problem, but they also have a solution in mind. A leader is a person who is dissatisfied with the ways things are. He has a burden, a vision, and a call to see something different. He wants to see something change, to build a new future. He then begins to communicate what he thinks, and where he wants to go. Nehemiah gives a "vision talk" to the troops. When he finishes they are ready for battle. He is able to motivate and enlist them by sharing that God's fingerprints are all over this vision, evidenced by the great answers to prayer and the generous offer of the king.

I believe that there are three aspects to leading:

1. Who the leader is: *Identity*
2. Where the leader is headed: *Inspiration*
3. How the leader brings others along: *Investment*

The first has to do with character traits such as genuine concern for people and the highest degree of integrity. The second has to do with an inspirational vision. The third has to do with the gifts and ability of the leader to invest in others by motivating, equipping and delegating responsibilities in order to facilitate reaching the desired destination. We will see all these aspects of leading unfold as the story continues.

I'm getting enthused just writing about this and seeing how what this leader did relates so clearly to my situation and, hopefully, to yours.

After reading this chapter, I wrote in my journal, "Lord, give me a positive, uplifting spirit, and the ability to inspire and motivate those I work with. Keep my vision clear and my motivation high."

QUESTIONS TO PONDER

In what way is the ability to inspire and motivate others a gift from God or a personality trait that you either have or don't have, as opposed to something that can be learned?

What is a leader to do if he/she is aware of all the problems and tends to focus on the difficulty of achieving the vision?

What kinds of things can a leader do in order to keep inspiration and motivation high and ongoing among the team?

05

Christian leaders understand to whom they belong, whom they serve, and who gives lasting success.

Nehemiah has just motivated his band of warriors (Nehemiah 2:18) and the response is unanimous: "Let us start rebuilding. So they began this good work."

As is the case with any true work of God, it will be criticized and this was no exception. "But when Sanballat the Horonite, Tobiah the Ammonite official and Geshem the Arab heard about it, they mocked and ridiculed us. 'What is this you are doing? Are you rebelling against the king?'" (Nehemiah 2:19)

I just love Nehemiah's response to this attack. He didn't cower. Fear didn't take over. He didn't hem and haw. He frankly and boldly declared, "The God of heaven will give us success. We his servants will start rebuilding."

It was very clear to Nehemiah that simply relying on his leadership skills would not carry the day. He understood at a profound and deep level that God was sovereign over the vision he gives. He understood that he and those on his team were, first and foremost, servants of the Lord. It was crystal clear to him that because of who the Lord was and their identity in him, they would succeed. "Not by might nor by power, but by my Spirit, says the Lord Almighty." (Zechariah 4:6 NIV)

Paul expresses a similar truth, "Last night an angel of the God *whose I am and whom I serve* stood beside me and said, 'Do not be afraid, Paul. You must stand trial before Caesar, and God has graciously given you the lives of all who sail with you." (Acts 27:23-24 NIV) Paul boldly declares that he belongs to God and serves God who is all-powerful!

I have a definition of leadership that I build on in my book, *Leaders Who Last*. In part, it reads, "A Christian leader is a humble, God-dependent, team-playing servant of God." This is so foundational to lasting Spirit-led success. It takes humility before the Lord as I use (but not rely on) my own skills or experience to achieve victory; totally depending on God for lasting results and not doing it by myself. Nehemiah says, *we* will build, not *I* will build. He clearly saw himself as part of a team that would accomplish the vision God had given.

David also shares such an understanding. "And David realized that *the Lord had made him king* over Israel and had made his kingdom great for the sake of His people Israel." (2 Samuel 5:12 NLT) God put him on the throne, not for David's sake, but for the people's sake. We see David grasping this truth early in his life as he encounters bears, lions, and Goliath. God has done it; God will accomplish it; God will deliver you into my hands. (This is quite a contrast to Saul who built a monument to himself.)

One of my favorite verses regarding David's God-glorifying and God-dependent attitude is 2 Samuel 5:20 (NLT), "So David went to Baal-Perazim and defeated the Philistines there. '*The Lord has done it*,' David exclaimed, 'He burst through my enemies like a raging flood!' So David named that place Baal-Perazim, which means 'The Lord who bursts through.'"

When I was in training with The Navigators and living in Los Angeles, I met Chuck and Marilyn Winter who had two sons, Brian and Steve. They were six and four at the time. One evening they invited me to dinner. The boys had been memorizing Bible verses and that night I asked Brian what his latest verse was. Without a moment's hesitation, he quoted his verse to me: "Not unto us, O Lord, not unto us, but unto thy name give glory, for thy mercy *and* for thy truth's sake." (Psalm 115:1 KJV)

I was a proud young man at that point in my life. It was all about me, what I was doing, what I was accomplishing. God used young Brian and that verse to cut through my pride and self-centeredness.

That night before I went to bed, I got down on my knees and confessed my sin to the Lord, asking for help in dealing with my pride. I often return to this verse in my times of worship and confession. As the song states, "I'm coming back to the heart of worship and it's all about you, it's all about you, Jesus. I'm sorry Lord for the thing I've made it when it's all about you."[5] Pride, self-sufficiency, and egocentricity drives and fuels so many leaders in the corporate world and, sad to say, in Christian circles as well.

Nehemiah has an important lesson for us. The God of Heaven will give us success. It's all about Him, about His glory, His purpose, His honor. I am *His* servant. He is not *my* servant to help me carry out my plans, my desires, my agenda in order to build my ministry with my people. It is fundamentally all about Him!

"So neither he who plants nor he who waters is anything, but only God who makes things grow." (1 Cor. 3:7 NIV)

QUESTIONS TO PONDER

Where can you identify pride and self-glorification in your ministry?

How have you defined success?

How is the Lord getting glory for the success you experience?

Honestly now, as people watch you operate, in what way does it lead to praising God, or is it leading to praising you for being so clever and gifted?

06

Leaders should expect opposition in various forms.

I was in a meeting in the early years of my ministry. The speaker made a statement that instantly jarred me into reality: "If you are a leader, expect to be misunderstood." I was young and idealistic. I thought my goals and dreams were so right that surely no one would falter or stumble in following along with me. Wow, was I ever wrong!

The "expect to be misunderstood" has expanded through the years to, expect to be: criticized, judged, called an ungodly leader, no leader at all, not a Christian, having no love for people…and the list goes on. Anyone who has had a leadership role for any length of time knows that being judged, condemned, or having one's motives questioned goes with the territory. If opposition comes only from perceived enemies of what you are trying to accomplish, that would be one thing. But in many cases it comes from some of your key people and that's especially hard to take. Enemy or close friend, having someone criticize you or your ideas is always difficult to receive and respond to. Once again, Nehemiah is a model for us.

In chapter two, Nehemiah is just getting under way with his vision and is immediately slammed. "But when Sanballat the Horonite, Tobiah the Ammonite official, and Geshem the Arab heard of it, they laughed at us and despised us, and said, 'What is this thing that you are doing? Will you rebel against the king?" (Nehemiah 2:19)

Nehemiah was:

1. Laughed at
2. Despised
3. Accused

A few verses later we see his response, "we will arise and build." (Nehemiah 2:20)

Former President Harry Truman said, "If you can't stand the heat, get out of the kitchen." Suffice it to say, when you are in the kitchen of leadership it can heat up. If everybody likes everything you're doing, you are probably not doing anything of significant value. Leaders don't lead and make decisions in order to be popular or appreciated. In Luke 6:26, we read,

> "There's trouble ahead when you live only for the approval of others, saying what flatters them, doing what indulges them. Popularity contests are not truth contests...your task is to be true, not popular." (*The Message*)

If Nehemiah wanted to be liked or well received by people in the area, he would never have decided to do what he did in the first place. Eric Geiger said, "If you want to keep everybody happy don't be a leader; sell ice cream." Nehemiah understood this.

He undertook the responsibility because he believed it was the right thing to do. It was the thing God wanted done. It was the thing that would be based on the promises of God. It was the thing that would bring honor to God. Leaders need to ask if it's right before asking if it's popular or even possible. Nehemiah is immediately criticized, has his motives judged, and he is ridiculed. This is just the beginning of opposition against him. We will see more of it later in the book.

In his book, *Well-Intentioned Dragons*[6], Marshall Shelley delineates some of the people types who will oppose your leadership and your decisions. Be on the lookout for them.

They are:

> 1. The Wet Blanket: No matter what the idea or decision on the table, Wet Blanket has a quiver full of reasons why it has never worked, will never work, and should not work because it is not the will of God
>
> 2. The Fickle Financier: If you do this or that, I will never give another dime to this ministry. Without my support and the support of my friends (who feel the same way I do) your ministry and leadership is dead in the water
>
> 3. The Sniper: Never seems to talk directly with a leader in a healthy manner voicing concerns, but rather stays at a safe distance and takes indirect pot shots in private conversations that paint the leader in a bad light
>
> 4. The Legalist: Has a list of absolutes that run from how much the leader paid for his house to how many verses should be sung from a particular song
>
> 5. The Merchant of Muck: The group gossip who disguises everything behind the mask of prayer requests and concerns

Do you recognize any people described here who are currently opposing what you and your leadership team are doing or dreaming of doing? Take courage from Nehemiah's response to the barrage of opposition,

"The God-of-heaven will make sure we succeed. We're his servants and we're going to work, rebuilding." (Nehemiah 2:20 *The Message*)

QUESTIONS TO PONDER

What kind of opposition or criticism are you currently dealing with?

How do you generally respond when you are attacked or criticized?

In what way can you put criticism, misunderstanding or personal attacks to good use?

07

Leaders artfully combine the spiritual and the human in getting the job done.

In the fourth chapter we find Nehemiah continuing to deal with opposition that began in chapter two. In Nehemiah 4:8 we read that plans are being laid to physically attack the people doing the work on the wall. Nehemiah could have called a halt to the work and transitioned into an all-day and all-night prayer meeting, asking the Lord for protection. Or, he could have redoubled his efforts and done everything within his power to fight the opposition. He didn't fall into the trap of either/or, but instead chose both/and. He combined the spiritual and the human, for we read in verse nine, "We prayed to our God and guarded the city day and night to protect ourselves." He prayed and guarded, not prayed *or* guarded.

I am reminded of two young girls who found themselves to be a bit late as they walked to school. One said, "We'll be late, let's stop and pray and ask the Lord to help us get there on time." "No," responded the other. "Let's run and pray that the Lord will help us get there on time." It seems to me that in most leadership issues it is always a matter of combining what God can do with what I can do. I can err on either side by trying (with human energy and gifting) to accomplish what only God can do or by trusting God to do what He is asking me to do.

A number of years ago I was chatting with a young man who was unemployed and praying for work. I saw him one Sunday at church and inquired how it was going. He responded by saying that he was not doing much but was simply resting in the Lord to be supplied with a job. I remember suggesting that there is a big difference between resting in the Lord and sleeping in the Lord.

I don't believe that resting, trusting, and believing are opposed to working, sweating, and trying. I don't think Nehemiah did either. Trusting is no substitute for hard work. Proverbs 3:5-6 talks about not leaning on your understanding; but I don't take that to mean that I shouldn't use my own understanding. I want to simultaneously lean on God and utilize my God-given ability. They are not contradictory but complementary.

Sometimes in leadership issues and decisions it's easy to over-spiritualize things and think that we just need to pray more. This can be a cop-out. Of course, we need to pray and trust; but does that eliminate the God-given responsibility to work hard, think well, and use all the gifts, strength, and wisdom that God supplies? A pastor once said that when he prayed, he prayed like it was all up to God and when he preached he preached like it was all up to him. That's the spirit we need to capture. For me, it is sometimes fear of failure and rejection that keeps me from moving out and giving my best effort. Fear causes me to spend an inordinate amount of time seeking God and asking him what I should do.

In many cases I don't need more information to know the will of God, but more courage to do the will of God. Good leaders have a bias for action and don't unnecessarily wait, operating out of fear masked as spirituality.

I have been in more leadership meetings than I can count where an issue was on the table and a decision clearly needed to be made. Fear won out and the leader went down the road of, "We need to pray more about this and trust God," as if trusting God meant we could not move ahead and make a decision. Sometimes waiting is the godly and wise thing to do and at other times it is the cowardly thing to do. We need wisdom to know the difference. The best leaders are those who carefully and prayerfully combine the best of both; they trust and wait, and they work and move.

QUESTIONS TO PONDER

What are some ways a leader could be overly spiritual in dealing with tough issues and decisions?

How can a leader be totally dependent and totally pro-active at the same time?

When would "waiting and trusting" be a cowardly act? A wise decision?

How would you determine if "faith" or "fear" is motivating your leadership actions and decisions?

08

Good Leaders are willing to confront people when necessary.

One of the responsibilities of a leader is to deal with conflict. The wise leader confronts people and issues head-on by considering various solutions and then acting prayerfully and decisively. Every good leader I have known and worked with has been willing to deal with issues and people and not run from them. The hardest types of issues are those that arise within the ranks of your followers, especially when they are in conflict with each other. Internal conflicts are rampant in leadership teams and among church members. Many leaders would rather move on than deal with such problems, especially when it involves your leadership team. Nehemiah takes a different approach.

In the fifth chapter of Nehemiah, we see a major conflict developing. In verses 1-5, Nehemiah hears that some of his leaders are charging interest to their poorer fellow countrymen and women, and also confiscating property when it can't be paid, thereby sending them to the poor house. He listens carefully to various reports of what is going on and then responds:

> "When I heard their outcry, and these charges, I was very angry. I pondered them in my mind and then accused the nobles and officials...I called together a large meeting to deal with them." (Nehemiah 5:6-7 NIV)

He then laid the issue on the table, spoke honestly with them and said,

> "What you are doing is not right...let the exacting of usury stop. Give back to them immediately their fields, vineyards, olive groves and houses and also the usury you are charging them...We will give it back they said...We will

do as you say. Then I summoned the priests and made the nobles and officials take an oath to do as they promised." (Nehemiah 5:9 NIV)

WOW! That is impressive! I see a process here:

1. He received information and facts
2. He had an emotional response to what he knew was wrong and had to stop
3. He gave some thought and pondered (perhaps thinking of the appropriate response)
4. He acted by confronting the guilty people and calling a meeting to deal with it openly
5. He pushed it through and got a firm commitment for action

Knowing Nehemiah as I do from studying this book, I believe that while he was thinking about what he heard and what needed to be done, he was also praying. You can't help but admire and respect such a leader. He had moral courage to confront what was not right and deal with people in a timely and thorough fashion. To be quite honest, I find this refreshing and very rare in leadership circles. Many leaders are devout cowards when it comes to confronting people, especially other leaders. Leaders are disqualifying themselves and dropping out today because of sin that nobody is willing to confront.

I have known and worked with leaders who would rather quit and move on rather than confront people. I recall a pastor I once worked with that was ready to leave the church because one elder was giving him a hard time. Rather than sitting down and confronting this elder, the pastor was doing everything he could (behind the scenes) to force the guy out, and if that didn't work, to leave himself. To confront this elder was something he just couldn't bring himself to do. I wonder when a leader "receives another call" how often it is due to the unwillingness to confront what needs to be confronted in the lives of people. A number of years ago I, along with some other leaders in my home church, crafted a statement regarding essential attributes of a small group leader.

One of the attributes is: "He is able to both challenge and encourage others." Many are up to encouraging, but how many are up to challenging, warning? Why is it so hard to "…exhort one another daily while it is called today, lest any of you be hardened through the deceitfulness of sin?"   (Hebrews 3:13)

The word exhort means to warn, admonish, urge, as well as encourage. But we can always hide behind, "Judge not lest you be judged," which is the scriptural cop out for those not wishing to confront sin in people, especially leaders. I would love to read a book on *The Lost Art of Confrontation.* Maybe we already have one; the book of Nehemiah!

QUESTIONS TO PONDER

How would you rate yourself on confronting people when it is clear you need to do it?

Is there an issue in the life of a particular person or leader that needs to be dealt with? What are you waiting for?

In what way can Nehemiah's example give you courage to do what you know needs to be done?

09

Leaders facilitate respect, understanding, and a genuine heart response to God's word.

In spite of all the hassles, setbacks, opposition and hard work, team-Nehemiah finishes the project and realizes the vision God gave from the get-go in chapter one. In Nehemiah 6:15-16 we read:

> "So the wall was completed on the twenty-fifth of Elul, in fifty-two days...this work had been done with the help of God."

Chapter seven is, for the most part, a cataloguing of various people who had a part in this amazing feat, along with a statistical accounting. In this chapter, we focus on what takes place in Nehemiah eight.

Chapter eight is one of my favorite chapters of the entire book. One theme that runs through the book is Nehemiah's God-dependence and his clinging to the promises of God, which are recorded in chapter one. He seems to be a man of The Book.

In chapter eight, Nehemiah's co-worker, Ezra, takes center stage to expose the people to the clear teaching of the Word of God. The chapter is insightfully instructive on how the Word of God can and should be presented to people and the effect it can have on people. Let's take a closer look at this wonderful chapter!

It seems to me that there are three phases to what we find in this chapter as it relates to the Word of God: Information, Understanding, and Application.

In verses 1-6, we see the people getting *information* from the Word of God:

> In verse one, they actually request to have the Word read to them. It was a team effort, as we

see in verse four. I always appreciate a plurality of leaders rather than one-man bands. In verse five, we notice the people standing, possibly showing their respect for the scriptures.

In verses 7-15, we see people *understanding* the Word of God:

The team helps people understand as they are instructed. The people grasp the meaning and weep as the truth sinks in. The second day scripture is again read, rapt attention is given and a clear opportunity to respond to the truth is presented.

In verses 16-18, we see people *applying* the Word of God:

Obedience takes place as people understand what God's will is for them. Read the chapter through for yourself and you can see a clear progression from: What does the Scripture say, to what does the Scripture mean, to what will we do with the Scripture?

Here are some basic conclusions I have drawn from Nehemiah 8 on attitudes and application of the Scriptures.

1. As people read or are taught God's Word, they need to travel from information, to understanding, to application.
2. Spiritual transformation occurs at the application level, not the information or understanding level. (See John 13:17) The Spirit of God changes people not because of what they "know" but because of what they "do" (with

God's help) with what they know.

3. Application should come as a result of prayer, thinking, and dialogue with others.

4. When God's Word is given and understanding is achieved, a response should be expected and asked for.

5. Helping people understand and apply God's word is best achieved in the context of teamwork: teachers, mentors, small group leaders, friends, and accountability partners.

Wow, what a chapter! Ancient, but *en pointe* and applicable.

I close this chapter with a quote from Randy Pope in his excellent book, *The Prevailing Church*. What follows is very pertinent to Nehemiah eight.

> "To aim at a Bible passage as one preaches, periodically making applications to personal life, will leave the believing community convinced they have been taught by God's man. But to aim at a personal life while preaching, bringing God's truth to bear upon its need, will leave the believing community convinced they have been taught by God's Spirit. Life-changing preaching does not talk to people about the Bible. Instead it talks to people about themselves. The basic principle in preaching is to give as much biblical information as the people need to understand the passage, and no more. Then move on to your application. I am discouraged to see how often intellectual stimulation is more desired than spiritual vitalization."[7]

QUESTIONS TO PONDER

As you consider everything in this chapter and reflect on your ministry, what can you do to better help your people move from information to understanding and then to life-transforming application?

Why does today's Christian teaching seem to spend so much time on information and so little time on application?

Personally, can you think of specific application you have made from hearing, reading, and studying God's Word, or are you falling into the trap of spending more time on information and understanding without allowing the truth in God's Word to transform you?

10

Leaders regularly rehearse organizational history and victories, reminding people of God's power, promises, character and faithfulness.

The project has been completed and Nehemiah is delighted; the obstacles have been overcome and Scriptures have been shared. Proverbs 13:19 reminds us that "A longing fulfilled is sweet to the soul." There is sweetness all around. We are now in Nehemiah 9 and we have a "history lesson" before us. The entire chapter is one long prayer that reviews God's dealing with the people of Israel, ending with a commitment to stay tight with God.

What a great lesson in leadership. People need to see the hand of God in their midst, they need to know God has been guiding their story. Our people need to be encouraged when they look back at some of the amazing things God has done. Sometimes we have short memories. We tend to focus on the negatives, the problems, the impossibilities. We (leaders and followers) easily forget that God is awesome, powerful and good for his word. It is powerful for leadership to often review what has been happening...the victories and accomplishments as well as the difficulties. In order for people to have hope for the future, they need to sense that their past and present contains bright moments with God.

When I am leading a meeting, small group or a leadership team, one of my favorite things to communicate is that *I am expecting God to act*. I base this on Psalm 42:11 (The Living Bible): "But O my soul, don't be discouraged. Don't be upset. Expect God to act! For I know that I shall again have plenty of reason to praise Him for all that He will do. He is my help! He is my God!"

One of the main reasons I expect Him to act now, and in the future, is because I regularly review what He has done in the past, which is what Nehemiah has done in chapter nine.

People need hope, they need to know and experience that "Jesus is the same yesterday today and forever." (Hebrews 13:8) Nehemiah 9 is the "yesterday" of God's dealings with the people of Israel that is being reviewed here.

Some years ago, I spent some time with a Christian leader who was considering the possibility of moving to Seattle where I was living at the time. He shared how the Lord had shown him special favor in getting a great rental car that he shouldn't have had. It was a small thing, but it bolstered his faith that God was leading him here. We talked about him sharing this later as he reviewed the process of God's leading in his relocation to Seattle. He is simply reviewing the history of God's dealings with him. This occurs here in chapter nine of Nehemiah as before in Nehemiah 2:18, "I also told them about the gracious hand of my God upon me and what the king had said to me." People get encouraged by reviewing the history of God's gracious activities in our midst.

As a leader, let me encourage you to regularly take time to allow people to see the fingerprints of God on things happening in the last week, month, or quarter.

QUESTIONS TO PONDER

How would reviewing what God has done affect your people?

What are a few awe-inspiring things the Lord has done in your group or organization in the last few months?

How could you, or will you, share with your people to encourage them?

11

Leaders help followers in establishing and maintaining commitments to God.

Well, we're almost finished with our study of this amazing and multifaceted leader. In this chapter we see him raising the bar and motivating the troops to stay on the high road of obedience, not compromising God's standard.

In the last verse of chapter nine we read, "Because of all this we make a firm covenant in writing; on the sealed document are the names of our princes, our Levites and our priests." (Nehemiah 9:38) This verse follows a lengthy review of God's dealings with the Jewish people over many years of history. It details how the Lord had given them promises, acted on their behalf and guided them through thick and thin. As the curtain rises on chapter ten, we see a list of people who sign on the dotted line, committing to reach for the high standard of God's desires and commands for them, both individually and corporately.

Nehemiah is well aware of what is at stake if disobedience to God's clear teaching is left unchallenged. He tells the people what God wants, gets them to sign on, and keeps the bar high. I see two issues raised in this tenth chapter.

Separation and Stewardship

Separation (verses 28-31): The Jewish people are reminded that they are unique. They should have different values and perspectives than the people around them. They were told over and over again throughout the Old Testament not to intermarry or adopt the practices of the people among whom they lived—especially not to worship their worthless gods.

Stewardship (verses 32-39): The Jewish people are reminded to give the best and the first to the Lord, both the firstborn and the first fruit. This is another thread that winds its way through the Old Testament: honoring God by giving Him their best.

The application for leaders is unmistakable. Whether we are thinking of a sports leader, a business leader, or a spiritual leader, we are always at our best when we are calling followers to their best, not letting them get away with sloppy standards and sloppy living. A leader should not be afraid to remind people what the organization or group values are and then hold followers accountable for those values. Nehemiah does this over and over. I think it is a principle that you get what you ask for. "If you ask for a small commitment, you will get a small commitment. If you ask for a big commitment, you will get a big commitment."

The late author Leroy Eims was fond of saying, "If you play a man's game, men will come to play." You will get the best that people have to offer when you expect the best from them. I believe this with all my heart. People want a cause bigger than themselves to live for and, if necessary, die for.

On October 20, 2004 in the Seattle Times, there was a great article about Michael Feiner, the former PepsiCo executive that personifies keeping the bar high. Here are a few excerpts from that article:

> "A slender man with disciplined posture, Fein-er has a sternness that tells people 'approach cautiously.' Yet for many of those who worked for him during his 20 years at PepsiCo, where he headed the personnel office, or who took his tough but popular management class at Columbia Business School, he's the boss they

want to emulate: fair, straightforward, ethical, demanding yet compassionate.

'"Mike has probably had more influence on shaping me as a professional and as an adult than probably any other single individual, says Dave Pace, Starbucks' human-resources chief who worked at Pepsi for 18 years. 'He was about values. He was about standards and he was about leading by example.'

"Feiner's proteges have gone on to head the HR departments at Dell, Microsoft and Sears. Harvard Business Review has published his advice. His new book, "The Feiner Points of Leadership' has landed on suggested reading lists for CEOs.

"Great bosses not only inspire and encourage, they hold employees as well as themselves accountable for meeting their expectations. Without measuring performance, the other leadership principles are toothless."

Perhaps Nehemiah was the Michael Feiner of his day. By holding them to a higher standard, he refused to let them get by with anything other than their best.

QUESTIONS TO PONDER

How are you doing in having clear and compelling values and standards for yourself and those you lead?

What are you doing that motivates and encourages your people to keep the bar high in their personal and professional life?

What will you start doing that you are not currently doing regarding values and standards?

12

**Leaders encourage their people
by celebrating and making a big
deal out of victories, creating joy,
enthusiasm, and high morale.**

Well, this is the end of our journey with Nehemiah. I trust you have profited as much from reading this book as I have enjoyed revisiting what I've learned and tried to apply.

Let's end by focusing on Nehemiah 12:27.

> "Now at the dedication of the wall of Jerusalem they sought out the Levites in all their places, to bring them to Jerusalem to celebrate the dedication with gladness, both with thanksgiving and singing with cymbals and stringed instruments and harps."

I would love to have been there on this day. They celebrated with gladness and thanksgiving; singing and playing musical instruments. I'll bet you could hear the joyful noise for miles. They had good reason to "party" with and for the Lord. Through ups and downs, through trials and tribulation, through tough decisions, and precarious moments, they finished what God had birthed in their hearts to do.

I love the song by Rita Baloche:

> *I will celebrate, sing unto the Lord; Sing to the Lord a new song.*
> *I will celebrate, sing unto the lord; Sing to the Lord a new song.*
> *With my heart rejoicing within,*
> *With my mind focused on Him,*
> *With my hands raised to the heavens,*
> *All I am worshipping Him.*[8]

One of the things good leaders do is make a big deal outof victories regardless of the size. Successful companies and churches value celebration and enjoy letting people know how much what they have accomplished is appreciated. Willow Creek Church in Chicago has "Attaboy Sundays" to celebrate the work of various people.

In an article titled "Vision Leaks," Pastor Andy Stanley from Atlanta has this to say about celebrating:

> "Many churches never stop to celebrate and they're missing a great, fun opportunity to reinforce the vision. Celebration is what puts skin on the vision. Nothing gives definition to vision like celebrating victories. Almost every Sunday we find a way to celebrate, hoot and holler, yell and scream. Once a year isn't enough. Spontaneously isn't enough. You must intentionally celebrate the vision over and over."

And I would add to Stanley's thoughts by saying it is imperative to celebrate all the good things that are happening all the time. I have worked for leaders who seldom have a word of thanks, appreciation, or celebration cross their lips. Perhaps the mindset is that people are only doing their jobs, what is expected of them, so why do they need to have praise and thanks heaped on them? Some take a negative step and add: it might even make them lazy and not work as hard or they might then expect a reward every time they turn around. Celebration is woven into the DNA of the Old and New Testaments. Every Jewish holiday is celebrating some great event in their history. They celebrate so they don't forget. Communion is a celebration.

I haven't seen many Christian leaders do a very good

job of "celebrating." We would do well to have "party money" in the budget to make a big deal over anything and everything. When I was on the pastoral staff of Our Savior's Community Church in Palm Springs, I pushed for having a special account to celebrate at any and all occasions with the people for whom I was responsible. Birthdays and anniversaries were noted and tangibly acknowledged. Encouraging cards were sent whenever I had the slightest reason to send one. One of my verses on this is I Peter 3:9 (The Message), "Instead bless! That's your job, to bless. You'll be a blessing and also get a blessing." I have discovered that one way I can bless people is to celebrate with them every chance that is offered to me.

People are starving for encouragement and affirmation. Followers are hungry for leaders to express appreciation and affirmation, but seldom hear it. Employees need it from their employers, kids need it from their parents, spouses need it from each other; but many don't hear enough celebratory words. We hear words when we mess up or don't come through as we should have or could have, but words of celebration and affirmation are strangely missing when we do something well. A sincere "thank you, I appreciated that" goes a long way. We can do better as leaders, we must do better as leaders!

With this no-celebration, no-appreciation attitude in mind, one of the saddest movies I ever saw was "The Rookie." It's a story about Jimmy Morris (played by Dennis Quaid) who had a really rough relationship with a dad who was in the military. They moved all the time and his dad cared nothing for his son's deep interest in playing professional baseball. Jimmy later tried to make it to the majors, but he seriously hurt his shoulder and had to drop out.

In the film we find him coaching a high school baseball team and teaching chemistry in a small Texas town. The team made a deal with him that if they won district he would try again to make the majors. Deal struck. They won and he tried out. As a pitcher, he was able, quite to everyone's surprise, to throw a baseball 98 miles an hour. To his amazement, (he was appreciably older than most major league players) he made it to the farm league and eventually to the majors.

When he was looking for affirmation from his dad (something he never got growing up), he heard: "Your grandfather used to say, 'It's okay to think about what you want to do until it's time to start doing what you were meant to do.'" Even at the end of the movie, after Jimmy had succeeded with his dream, his dad still could not bring himself to "celebrate" with Jimmy. You could see the pain written all over Jimmy's face when they had a last meeting. His dad just stood there, seemingly unable to say "I love you, great job, I'm proud of you, I was wrong, I'm sorry, I rejoice with you over your accomplishments," or anything of any substance. As I watched the movie I felt like screaming at his dad: "Do something, say something, celebrate, get happy; rejoice with your son. He is desperate for your approval and love." But, nothing!

Don't let that be the legacy you leave your family and friends. Be a positive, encouraging, affirming and loving influence to the glory of God!

QUESTIONS TO PONDER

What are some small victories that you could celebrate in your family, ministry, work, or small group?

What are some creative and unconventional ways to call attention to personal and corporate victories that would build morale and vision and that would simply encourage people?

Beyond Nehemiah, what other scriptural examples of celebration come to mind?

CONCLUSION

We have studied, admired, and learned from Nehemiah as we observed his gutsy and God-honoring leadership. He received a clear vision from God, put that vision into action by asking and believing big, formed a team, and began to see that vision become reality. We have seen him face opposition from within and without, deal with significant setbacks, rally the troops and keep them motivated and inspired. And here's the best part, this awesome work was completed in 52 days! Who wouldn't want to emulate this incredible leader?

He truly exemplifies all the best in leadership; he's bold, courageous, confrontational (when it's called for), and persistent in sticking with what he feels led to do. In my estimation, the book of Nehemiah is the best book of the Bible to study and learn exemplary leadership.

You have traveled with me as we have explored twelve aspects of his leadership. You have received lots of information. Now it's time to turn that information into application. Now it's time ask what, with God's help, you will do to begin to apply what you have learned from Nehemiah.

Here are some suggestions to get you started:

1. Write down the twelve leadership lessons so you have easy access to them as you pray over them and evaluate how you are doing on a personal level.
2. Take each of the twelve chapters and make them discussion topics for your leadership, pastor or staff team.

3. Have a team evaluation on how you would rank how you are doing on each of the twelve.

4. Develop a game plan on one to three of them, turning them into specific goals for a period of six months to a year

The Christian church is in desperate need of leadership. Everywhere I turn the cry is for more leaders. We need more leaders like Nehemiah, who lead by following God's leadership. As you are led by him, empowered by him, and honor him, may you be one of these modern-day Nehemiahs as, together, we seek to build His church and advance the gospel to all nations.

ABOUT THE AUTHOR

Dave was born in Los Angeles and spent his growing up years in Palm Springs, California. His family is Jewish so it was a surprise to many people at the Palm Springs Community Church when Dave showed up after a co-worker had shared the gospel with him. After three months of reading, thinking and asking a ton of questions, he was wonderfully saved and transformed at an evangelistic youth night.

He is forever grateful to the Lord Jesus for saving him and for the many wonderful people that prayed for him, sharing solid doctrine as well as books to guide him in his spiritual growth. Dave hasn't slowed down in his fifty-five years as a Christ-follower…he has no intention of doing so!

Two years after becoming a Christian, Dave was introduced to The Navigators and soon became involved in training with them; eventually becoming Navigator staff. Dave and Susan were married the same year (1968) that he left the market place and begin working with The Navigators. He remained on Navigator staff for 37 years; living and serving in both Northern and Southern California, Colorado, Washington State and eight years in Sweden as a missionary to university students as well as working with local churches.

Dave honed his communication and leadership skills by being an active member of Toastmasters International for 18 years and achieved the highest level possible; that of Distinguished Toastmaster.

In 2005 Dave retired from The Navigators and began professionally coaching. He now has his own website and coaching business. You can find him and all his free content at www.davekraft.org

He has had the joy of coaching several hundred pastors around the world, over the phone. After leaving The Navigators, Dave also served as a pastor for eight years with Mars Hill Church based in Seattle.

Dave wrote "*Leaders Who Last*" in 2010 and "*Mistakes Leaders Make*" in 2012, and has had the joy of conducting seminars all over the world based on both books. Dave and Susan have been married for 48 years and are the parents of four adult children and the grandparents of seven grandchildren. Dave is an avid reader, loves music and movies and likes to take on the younger dudes in racquetball.

NOTES

[1]Blackaby, H. (2008). Experiencing God. Nashville, TN: B&H Books.

[2]Adapted from a Web article by Pastor Rick Warren. *3 Aspects of the Vision God has for Your Church.* August 22, 2013. www.pastors.com

[3]Collins, J.C. (2001). Good to great. Why some companies make the leap—and others don't. New York, NY: HarperBusiness.

[4]Campbell, D. (1990). If you don't know where you are going, you will probably end up somewhere else. Chicago, IL: The Thomas More Association.

[5]Lyric from "Heart of Worship" by Matt Redman

[6]Shelly, M. (1994). Well-intentioned dragons: Ministering to problem people in the church. Ada, MI: Bethany House Publishers.

[7]Pope, R. (2001). The Prevailing church. Chicago, IL: Moody Publishers.

[8]Lyrics from "I will Celebrate" by Rita Baloche

DAVEKRAFT.ORG

Made in the USA
San Bernardino, CA
15 November 2016